50 Original Monologues

&

Tips For Success

by Steven G. Lowe

THIS BOOK IS DEDICATED TO

Joseph T. Lowe, Sr. and Frances Helen Lowe
for your loving support.

SPECIAL DEDICATION

Rick Lowe
Tammy Lowe-Martino

SPECIAL THANKS

Kathleen Rushall
Ryan Tsang
C. Anthony Chase
Colleen Couron-Smith
and all the actors at The Actors Room

Copyright © 2011 by Steven G. Lowe

Cover by Zachary DiPego

ISBN 978-0-615-59382-1

Manufactured in the United States of America
First Edition November 2011

CONTENTS

CHAPTER THREE - SHOW ME SOMETHING
20 TO 30 SECOND MONOLOGUES

CHAPTER FOUR - QUICK... BUT EFFECTIVE
30 TO 60 SECOND MONOLOGUES

Chapter 1

Range and Depth Required

Approximately 1.5 to 2-Minute Monologues

Explanation:

Monologues of this length are most commonly requested and a good piece for the actor to show both range and depth. Keeping in mind, "range" represents the variance of your ability to portray different characters; "depth" represents the intensity, strength and complexity of feeling, emotion and profundity of the character. All the same rules apply, as any great monologue must encompass relevant choices and emotional involvement, which carries the weight of the words. There's a bit of breathing room to develop the character (mannerism, subtleties, etc.) so, have some fun... but remember to keep your choices clear and consistent without overpowering the dialogue.

 **Tip!** Energy, energy, energy!! There are a few reliable areas where actors can go to help themselves... none more effective than energy. Use of the four energies (Face, Body, Voice and Emotion) will breathe life into the character and the moment. Being one-dimensional is boring and lifeless. A scene without energy is like a balloon without air... It has yet to reach its full ability and beauty. So, don't be afraid to get verbally, physically and emotionally involved... risk and you will be rewarded!

No one will ever help you the way you can help yourself
- Steven G. Lowe

"Outcast"

Hey. I'd introduce myself but you probably already know me...
I'm sure you've seen me around. I'm pretty popular like that. I
have lots of friends. We hang out everyday; we spend all kinds of
quality time together. I hide but they always seem to find me...
just like you. Hell, just the other day we... (face energy
recognizing they don't remember) yeah, we - you and I, were
hangin out in the field at school... while all your buddies held me
down and you shoved grass and dirt in my mouth. And there was
the time you nearly raped me... (swallowing hard, tearing up)
you took off all my clothes, beat me up and left me naked in the
bathroom. You don't remember? That one was hard to forget.
Hmm... okay, then what about the time when you smeared dog
crap on my clothes and told everyone in the school. That was
good for a few laughs. Everyone was laughing. Remember?

I went home and contemplated suicide that night. My parents
were watching TV down stairs. They thought I was talking on
facebook with all of my "friends". I love my parents... they're just
a little out of touch. Best two out of three... one more "heads"
and I wouldn't be standing here right now... not that you'd notice.
Well, maybe that's not true... what would you do for laughs?
(angering) How would you feel superior or in control without me?
You may think I don't matter... but I do! I fill a very important
need... a void... as long as you're tormenting me the others are
safe for another day. You still look a little confused. Maybe I
should introduce myself after all... I'm "Ugly", "Crap For Brains",
"Zit Face", "Fat-Ass", "Dumb-Ass", Four-Eyes", "Geek", "Ginger",
"Homo", "Retard", "Loser", "Loser", loser... I'm shit.

"Here I Am"

So, here I am. You're always asking me to let you in, to tell you how I feel. Okay, where do you want me to start? What do you want to know? You want to know that I'm angry? I am very angry. Or... or how about that I hurt? You want to know about that? I hurt so deep, that I ache... And I don't know if it's my anger that hurts me or if it's my hurt that makes me so angry. Instead, I ignore it... I just ignore it. And that makes me "feel", I feel empty and that's the worst feeling of all.

You want me to talk? Are you sure? Because if I tell you that I'm angry and hurting and empty, what are you going to do about it? Huh? If you're gonna ask someone to let you in... really let you in, you better be ready to handle it... because it's not fair to make me stand here and spill out my feelings if you're not ready to help.

"Cyber Diet"

So, I don't eat. Big deal. I don't have anorexia! Why is it that every girl who doesn't eat like a cow has to have an eating disorder? Do you have any idea how hard it is to stay popular these days?

My mom spews advice but she doesn't know... she only had to compete with the girls at her school. I wish it were that easy! I'm up against the Internet... the whole fricking world. Every sleaze out there who finally figured out how to turn on a computer is competition "Oh, power on... now flirt!" (mocking giggle).

If you have one extra pound - you're out, no "top eight" for you! Oh, and if you're not putting out because you want to "save yourself" well, then you better look flawless or else you're... unnoticed. And I don't think I could handle being invisible on cyberspace and at home. So, pass the carrot stick and bring me the size "one!"

"Final Rest"

I haven't been sleeping again. I've been waking up in the middle of the night feeling… lonely, feeling sad, and… empty. I then do what comes naturally for me… I lie there and over-think my current situation. I start to think about my life and how everything hasn't exactly gone as "planned". So, depending on the kind of day I've had, I get angry and frustrated. Sometimes, just to mix it up, I become frustrated then angry… but mostly I cry. I cry a lot.

I know what you're going to say; "It's been over two years. I need to move on". Well, I've tried that… She won't leave, she's in everything I do, everything I own, everywhere I go. We shared everything! Where could I "move on" so that my memories of her, my love for her wouldn't be? I don't exist without her. So, I've made a decision. Want to hear what it is? Well, you probably won't but you don't have a choice… I'm commandeering my own future. I'm taking back the control. Ah, hell, I'm going to kill myself! I hope you'll understand; but I'll settle for your forgiveness. I'm so tired.

"Thinking Positive"

You know... I'm frustrated right now, feeling a little down. But you can't tell because I'm not supposed to be... because nobody likes being around someone that's negative. Just ask my ex. It's not "in" right now. Don't even mention the word "Negative". Be positive! Keep it all inside... lie to yourself and everyone around you. Don't wanna impose on anyone's good time with my painful and possibly suicidal thoughts.

So, I'm happy... see (smiling big). I smile even though the love of my life left me, I lost my job and I've been sick for months... but I got an angle on that. I played it smart. See, I couldn't get health insurance and since our opportunistic, thieving government forces me to get raped by my auto insurance company, I crashed my car... for the medical coverage to kick in. It all makes perfect sense, especially when you're depressed. "Hey Doc, while you're fixing my smashed face, could you also take a look at the lingering cough I have.... make sure I didn't develop pneumonia in the accident or something? Yeah thanks!" Something about sticking it to the man does bring a smile to my face... even if it still hurts. I'm thinking positive!

"Pain"

Pain... what an interesting, ugly little word. So conceited and angry. It doesn't even need two syllables to get your attention; it packs all of its power into just one, tiny, profound four-letter word. I'm trying to stay focused but I'm a little... bewildered, I guess. I'm usually a very rational thinker but this, this kinda snuck up on me... like a seal being clubbed in the head. It's a lot to process. So, I'm stuck, how do you out think pain? There're so many variations one of them is bound to get you, right? Right?

Anyway, doesn't matter, I'm not looking for company in my misery, you couldn't match mine... not today. This isn't your ordinary, everyday - paper cut or broken bone type of pain... nope. This isn't "Hey, look at me hurting, my significant other left me" kinda crap. This one should have come with a warning sign. (beat) Just hours before everything was fine, life was crusin' along and I was happy. I should have known. (tears well up) Maybe that was the sign I missed. (shrugging shoulders) Then pain happened and life as I knew it... (sigh)... it became really personal.

So, I just need to make sense of it because I figure once I understand how it works... (sigh/beat). It just shouldn't hurt this bad. I'm stronger than this. I am way more shallow than this! Aww, man! I hate you "Hope" you're a liar. At least "Pain" doesn't make you believe everything's gonna be okay. Yeah, I know that's not very logical of me. Oh well. I buried my self-respect today, just gave it away. It's hurting a lot worse than I thought it would.

"Boundaries - The Last Stand"

It feels like everyone I know has lost their minds. Nothing seems to matter or make sense anymore. It's like they don't care. No one says what they mean, no one does what they say. It's frickin impossible to keep up or count on anyone! I'm starting to get angry… and a little self-conscious. It's like I'm in rejection purgatory but if I say anything then I'm just being sensitive or they make me feel stupid for being dramatic. I should matter to you. Just say whatever the hell it is you mean and stick to it! That's all I'm saying… and I'm not crying about it, see no tears!

Oh, and no one listens either… to me in particular. My friends, my family, the idiot at the drive-through window… seriously everyone, it's like a conspiracy to make me feel insignificant. I don't want to "Super-Size"! Stop trying to force-feed me calories. Have I done something wrong? Just tell me! Am I really just "overreacting" or am I the only sane one left?

My parents, uh my parents… they don't say much that matters but I did pick up on one nugget of truth, "Set boundaries. There's nothing wrong with wanting to be respected". Amen to that, my clueless 'rents! So we're clear, I'm only gonna care a little while longer… (beat, tears) there you got the tears, happy?! My word still means something… even if yours doesn't. And I mean it. That's kinda repetitive… but whatever.

"Memories & Pain"

I close my eyes sometimes and sit, just sit trying to "be" with nothing in my head at all. The silence is so beautiful. Then it starts. It all comes rushing in; like a song I haven't heard in a while. All my dreams, (down inflection) my hopes, (smile - up inflection) and the good times we had. Where did it all go? (insignificant chuckle) Wow, I was invincible and invisible with nothing but life to conquer ahead of me... all the memories. (emotional transition - angry) They mock the life I have now. Coming to me in songs and smells and places I'll never see... they haunt me. Memories... they're everywhere but where I want them to be! Get out of my head and leave me alone now! (beat) I just want a little silence from my thoughts... Just for a minute. Is a minute too much to ask?

"How Did This Happen (Female)"

Oh no... what did I do? How did this happen? This is a nightmare. My life is over. Everything is all wrong. My hopes and dreams are over. How do I stop this? God please don't let this happen to me. Please! I promise I'll never do it again... I'll, I'll do whatever it takes... if you just stop this from happening. I'm too young to have a baby. I don't want to be a mom yet... maybe after I'm married... I don't know. I'm too young to know. (crying) Everyone I know is having sex... why did this have to happen to me? I just want to wake up! (crying harder) Oh no, what will I tell my parents? This is bad. After all the warnings. My daddy... he's going to think I'm a slut. Everyone at school is going to see. This was supposed to be special... now I'm just gonna look like a hoe! I don't want to feel like this anymore. (crying stops - regaining composure) I need some advice... you're my friend, say something. Are you there? Never mind. I'm just going to call him... he loves me. Braden's a good person; I know he'll understand. We can make a good home for our baby. He'll provide for us... (smiling) we'll run away together and it'll all be fine. It might even be fun. I love him. He'll understand... he loves me.

"My Headphones"

(headphones on, gun held against his/her head - from profile turn straight-ahead, into the moment) - Ah man. Crap! (lowering gun) Not good. (pull headphones off, moving them to the neck) How many times I gotta tell you to knock little bro? How'd you reach the doorknob anyway? How long you been standing there? Huh? Come here. Come on! Don't be scared. (waving gun slightly) This ain't nothin'. Here look I'll put it away. Okay? I didn't mean for you to see all that. (3 beat, looking around) Hear that? No you can't... haha! That's because it's MY private party. (take headphones off and admire) Just the way I like it; no outside noise and that's important... know that. When I put these on (beat) I disappear. You'll see one day. When you get older your music's gonna matter. It blocks out the bad stuff that hurts your soul... I swear, sometimes it's all I got. When things start gettin' crazy these go on. They're all that matters to me... besides you. I can listen all day to my music. (beat, deep breath) They haven't been blocking out the noise lately, not like they used to. Here, maybe they'll work better for you. I want you to have these. Where you goin'?! And just like that. (beat - looking the headphones over - putting them on) Maybe I'll give'em another try.

"How Did This Happen (Male)"

Oh no… what did I do? How did this happen? This is a nightmare. My life is over. Everything is all wrong. My hopes and dreams are over. How do I stop this? God please don't let this happen to me. Please! (crying) I promise I'll never do it again… I'll, I'll do whatever it takes… if you just stop this from happening. I'm too young to be a parent. I don't want a kid yet… maybe ever… I don't know. I'm too young to know that kinda stuff. Everyone I know is having sex… so, why did this have to happen to me? I don't deserve this! I wish I could wake up! (crying subsides) My parents are gonna kick me out. Not that they're much better. They had me the same way. Mistakes happen. Whatever, Josh's mom likes me… I'll crash at his place. They're pretty chill. Now everyone at school's gonna see… she'll probably show her stomach off to everyone all proud that I did her. I don't care just proof positive that I'm a playa. (laughs). How could I let this happen? I'm done feelin' like this! I need some advice… you're my friend, say something. Are you there? Never mind. I just won't return her psychotic calls. I'll stay away form her. (angry) She probably did it on purpose… she set me up. It's probably not even mine. How do I know who else she slept with… she slept with me. Right? Man this sucks.

"Addiction"

I was up all night thinking about you again. I promised myself I wouldn't do that. I tried, I really did. I thought I was losing my mind. I didn't go to work, again. I wouldn't have gotten anything done anyway. I can't think clearly... you're in my head like nothing I've ever known. You're all I seem to think about anymore. I know it's wrong to obsess like this... I know I must look desperate... pathetic. You may have noticed, my friends have stopped coming around... people are starting to stare. Some kid even pointed at me the other day in the store but I don't care. I love you more than life itself. Nothing else matters when we're together. I belong. You make me feel so good and warm and, and... (pulling on face) I want to feel that way all the time... (tears) but I feel horrible today! My insides hurt they're churning! You're hurting me! You always want more... you want too much. There's nothing left of me anymore. I have no self-respect. I considered hurting someone today, you know? I wanted to so bad... because of you! I have to leave you. I have to leave you. I have to leave you! I know that now. I'm so weak! I'm going to be strong today... I want to be strong. I need help.

"Not Done Yet"

I've never felt this good in my life! Seriously, my stomach is weird with feelings I haven't felt in years. I want to jump for joy... stay tuned for that development. It's like everything good rolled into one. (deep, cleansing breath) I've waited years for this day to come. You know better than anyone; my life's been a series of letdowns and mistake, so many incredibly stupid mistakes, really just a disaster. (laughing) It's been awful. I hated every breath I was forced to take... but I never blamed the four winds or the other shoe... no matter how many times it dropped. It got ugly sometimes, and trust me, God and I had words... harsh words... but I never asked "Why me?" I knew why... lives had to be touched. Lives that weren't done yet, and I'm not being conceited or bragging but I never give up. That's why. You always put your strongest player in the game. After the accident I never gave up. My parents didn't raise a victim or a quitter. I was equipped... I could handle it. No matter how many times I wanted to disappear... I'm still here and that's what matters. Right?

I may have sat in this chair pissed off but I kept saying life doesn't end this way for me! It didn't start this way and it won't end this way. Nothings over until I give up... I'm in control of that, no one else. Life is good today. Isn't it wonderful? Look... (tearing up - looking down at your finger) it moves... it moved this morning. Thank you Lord! I have my rhythm back Doc! (tapping the finger against the leg as if to the beat of music). I can feel the song coming back to my body. I'm getting out of this chair... I'm not done yet.

"Tilt"

I know that look... I know what you're thinking, but you're wrong. I'm not okay. Not even close. So don't look at me like everything is fine. Stop telling the doctor lies... you do know why I'm stressed. I'm not "Fine" I - am - under a lot of pressure! I need medication! Please, I'm begging you please, accept that there's something wrong with me. I need you to acknowledge that. "Note it" in your journal or whatever it is you have to do. Pencil my illness in. I need you to hear me. Your daughter isn't the perfect picture of health. I'm sorry for the inconvenience! And stop making me apologize for it! Poor old Norman Rockwell's rolling over in his grave... the Smith family isn't picture perfect. They pulled a 3-pound ball of hair out of my stomach today. That's not normal. I've got more bald spots than Grandma. I've bitten all my nails off... if I could reach my toes they'd be gone too. I've chewed off my weight in skin, years of eating skin like comfort food... I bleed. (tearing up) I bleed, Mom. When do I get to stop paying for yours and Dad's marriage... and all the other screwed up things you've done to yourselves? Huh? It's not my fault that Dad has his life outside our home... I miss him too. Get some counseling or divorce his cheating, ungrateful ass and move on. Just make a decision already! Because if you both don't get it together soon... I'm not going to be able to hold on. I'm slipping here. This is a very overt cry for help! No secrets here. Get a frickin clue. (beat) I'm checking out of here. (beat - chewing on her hair) You coming?

"Surprise!"

(blindfolded, arms behind back as if tied - waking up) - Hello? What the... okay, what's going on? (beat) Is someone there? You guys are really funny. Hahaha! James! Dude seriously... I'm gonna kill you man! Come on the fun's over. The blood circulation is cutting off in my hands... not cool. Why the hell am I blindfolded? Ah man, this blindfold better not be your dirty underwear again. What the hell is your fixation with dirty underwear and my face? I'm getting angry! Untie me or I'll tell Amanda your cheating on her with that blond chick from the club... see how funny you think that is. She's hot... I'd break up with Julie for a piece of that... or her friend. No joke. (beat) Hello?! Where am I?

Heeeellooo?! I can hear you... I know you're there. Why are you doing this to me? (scared) James? Please... speak to me. Who are you? This isn't fun anymore... I'm really starting to freak out here. Seriously! Do I know you? Why are you doing this to me? Oh crap. Is it you Ryan? Ryan? Look man we were just being stupid. Dude, it was just stupid drunken fun. It wasn't personal. I mean, come on... it's not like we trashed your house... I'll clean your car. My brother paints cars he'll repaint it. I'm sorry, okay? Just don't hit me... I'm, I'm very, very sorry... James did most of it. I mostly watched I swear on my mother's grave. Uh, all right this is crazy! I want to be untied now! I mean it! (starting to cry) Just tell me your name, will you do that for me? I have to pee. I want to know your name. We can be friends. I'll do anything you ask... seriously anything! Wait! What are you doing?! Oh, okay thank you, thank you so much. (bringing hands forward, as if untied - then remove the blindfold - beat - eyes widen, mouth drops open) My birthday. Wow... hey James... you crazy, you guys really got me (forced laugh)... Surprise! Hahaha. Hey there's Amanda and God... Julie... I was just messing with you... cause I knew it was you guys. I'm really sorry.

"Oops, I'm Sorry"

I heard the news today... about the accident. What were you thinking letting Mom behind the wheel? And I'm even more amazed you got in. (beat) Mom, Dad... or Dad and Mom... I don't want either of you to think I care more for the other based on the order of names. (slight sad laugh) Okay, this is a lot harder than I thought it would be... shocker, huh? It's always been so hard for me to talk to you both. No blame... it was all me. No argument there huh Dad? God knows you tried. Wasn't my strong suit. (beat) You were great parents... I was lucky. So, I know I wasn't always the greatest son (daughter) far from it, actually... but you always loved me just the same. It makes this even harder to write. I wish I had done more to show you I loved you. I wish I could have just taken out the trash a few more times, washed the car... or come home on time. I'm so sorry I didn't... (starts to cry) hug you more. Seems so simple now. But as Mom always used to say, "That's water under the bridge." (beat) Except see that's the problem, it's not. This pain is very real, it's right here in my heart. It's so painful, my chest aches and you're not here to rescue me. You always knew how to make me feel safe. That seemed to be the only way I knew how to get close... always on my terms. Anyway, surprise, I was listening and I needed it... even if I didn't know it at the time.

I had so many chances, why didn't I just say it? What's wrong with me that I couldn't say thank you or I love you... or oops, I'm sorry that I screwed up your lives? I did. No one wants to see their child go through what I, what we went through. What I put you through. You just wanted me to be normal... happy. Truth be told, I'm not mad at you. I would have left me too. I know; too soon, right? You know you're up there laughing. (beat) I was a stupid kid that didn't know what he (she) had. Well, no more excuses; I love you, I'll miss you, and by-the -way, oops, I'm really sorry for everything. Better late than never, huh Dad? Hug Mom for me. Rest well... your grateful son (daughter), Jesse.

"Missing"

(bewildered scared and anxious) - I don't know what happened.
I've told you already! How many more times do I have to say it?
You're wasting time! (beat) I'm sorry… I'm scared. We, Joshy
and I, were in the produce section… he was standing right next
to me. I was picking out some damned apples. He won't eat the
bruised ones. When I put them in the basket he was gone.
(tearing up) I looked around and I yelled for him. He was right
there with me the entire time, I swear. I'm not a bad mother. I
always watch so closely. My husband even nags me about it -
"He's going to be a sissy if you keep suffocating him." Well, now
he's gone! (tears start to flow). Oh my God. My husband, he
doesn't know. I have to call him. I have to tell him I lost our son
(crying). This can't be happening. I have to sit down. You have to
find my Joshy. He's so small and shy. He wouldn't have
wandered off like this. (epiphany) Oh no… someone has him. Oh
no, oh no… they're going to hurt my baby. I'm going to be sick.
(gagging, covering her mouth) My baby's out there, (crying) he
needs my help and I can't help him. Some sick bastard has my
child and you're not helping me! Find my son! Please help me
find my son.

Chapter 2

Life Is Messy

Approximately 2.5 to 3.5-Minute Monologues

Explanation:
Messy is fun... out of the box! Monologues of this length give you time to be messy in a creative, purposeful and relevant way. This type of extended monologue explores and showcases your range, depth, character choices (be interesting!) and ability to sustain a moment. Strong transitions are also key to making it work. A coach may request a monologue of this size to help the actor work through personal hang-ups and anxieties. There's real work to be done, so don't become comfortable or lazy. No script is written with wasting time in mind. Monologues are "stand-alone" pieces meant to entertain, inspire, move, and "Wow" us. It's the actor's responsibility and freedom to orchestrate such a moment to messy perfection. Step out of your safety zone and do something meaningful and memorable.

Tip! When creating a "moment", chemistry is crucial. An actor will often accomplish this task with eye contact, physical positioning, and touch, among other choices. A monologue is very personal, and likely to be without the support of common scene chemistry (two or more actors), as you will be standing alone. Some simple rules of engagement should be applied: a) Know who or what your character is speaking to before you start. b) Know what your character's "motivation" is or simply put, what they want. c) Know your endgame! I call this your "target". What do you want the audience to believe about your character when you're done? d) Draw the audience in by finding ways for them to relate or identify. They must *care* or *feel*

something about your character for it to be meaningful, for them to truly connect. If you can suspend disbelief for your audience, you have effectively achieved a chemistry-driven moment.

The quickest way to get out of your head is to believe your heart
- Steven G. Lowe

"Merciful Knife"

So, what if I told you that I killed someone? Would that shock you? You'd probably think I was crazy, right? That's okay... I'd think the same thing. But you didn't live my life, the life my family had to live. They counted on me and he would do "things", horrible "things"... He'd look at me while he was doing... "things"... and just smile with those yellow teeth. I wasn't afraid of him. He thought I was but... but I was just a kid. I mean what could I do, right?

So, on my ninth birthday he got me this really cool pearl-handled knife. I remember thinking, "I'm gonna do big things with this knife." I loved it. It was one of the only times I ever hugged him. Well, he came home one night, a couple years later and was really raring up for a "good time". I wasn't scared but I was shaking. He went through my mom and at my sister with a rage I've never seen in a human before or since. She tried to scream but nothing came out and he... he, snapped her, just snapped her... like a tiny little twig.

They were counting on me. So, everything went, um, dark... yeah, dark. When it all stopped spinning... I looked down at my knife, the pearl handle was covered in blood... his blood. He looked up at me and I looked back at him but he wasn't grinning anymore. I stuck him in the throat. The way I see it; I was merciful. I wanted him to die quick... cause he was my dad.

"My Little Miracle"

My mind has never been clearer, my purpose more defined...
then it was today. I held in my hands, for the first time, a life that
mattered to me. One I didn't want to take. I'm not a good man...
God knows I've had my issues. My daughter was born today.
Oh, I'm so proud. I grew tall today. I stared down at her beautiful
little face and I saw she was trying to look back at me... their
eyes don't open very wide you know... but I knew she saw me.
She was checkin' things out for sure. Tears of happiness man...
and I haven't had a reason to cry for a while, trust that. I was a
dad.

I placed my hand on her tiny chest... I never realized what my
hand looked like before that moment. The same hands that did
crazy, evil things were holding something so fragile and
precious. But just like that (heavy crying starts) her tiny heartbeat
stopped. I couldn't feel it anymore. I thought did I break her? I
started screaming for help. Hey, hey somebody help! Help me!
Help my little girl... please. (beat) Everyone came running in...
they took my little girl from me. I told her, "Daddy's here
sweetheart!" I was gonna tell her be strong like your father...
(crying stops) but I realized I was just as helpless. Helpless as a
baby, as the lives I took. The people I hurt. And it hit me.

No you don't! Please don't do this to me... to her. To her! Kill me
instead! What can I do? Tell me! Please, how can I fix this? I'm
sorry. (beat) And then I heard it, the most amazing sound I'll ever
hear... a still small beep... and another and another. The
monitor... my baby's heart started and was strong. It was a
miracle... my little miracle. I won't forget... life changed today.

"Hope For A Better Past"

I don't hope for a new car or... more money, not anymore. What I want is to wake up somewhere free of the sins I've committed. The weight lifted from the mistakes I've made. I want some separation from stress, worry and pain. (vocal sigh of relief) I want to feel like everything is new again. That would be an amazing day. The view from that mountaintop would be incredible. I'd look out over my life seeing only the good I've done, the smiles I've caused... the people I've helped, maybe stopped to hug or compliment. The challenges are fine too... I don't mind the challenges but I'd only want to remember the victories. Hey, it's my perfect place, okay? Just the victories... that's all.

There are things I can't change... some I won't change. Seriously, when I really stop to think about it... why didn't someone tell me the cost; the horrible guilt... the loss I'd feel? Choices matter! The cost is so high. Didn't anyone love me enough to warn me? Was I not listening? They should have made me listen. God help me! (tears) I want to matter to myself again. Leave the bad behind. I want to hope again in these last minutes.

(gaining composure/strength) Well, it's too late now. My last words seem so weak... they have no impact. Who cares? (beat) I'm truly sorry... but you may never know it. If I had another life to give I would but this is all I have for them to take. Sorry... hmm, so easy to say now. Ever want to just get away from the life you've made? Is there even such a place?

"A Fish Story"

When I was younger my dad and I used to go fishing... I miss those times. He'd wake me up and say, "Let's go! The fish can't eat until we get there!" I don't know why but I laughed every time he said it... I think that's why he did it. It's like it was yesterday... the sun was just coming up, slight chill in the air... God, I loved it. We would sit there for hours sometimes, and never catch a thing. But it was okay, because I was with my dad.

Then one day, BAM! I get this huge tug on my line. I didn't know what to do! I think we were both surprised... there were actual fish in this pond after all. So, my dad grabbed hold of my shoulder and said, "Don't let go! Let's give your Mom something to clean." So, I fought with that fish... I wasn't about to let this one get away. After what seemed like an hour, I finally reeled that sucker in. It was beautiful. It was about this big (large hand gesture); well, maybe more like this big (smaller gesture).

Anyway, that's the thing about a good fish story the fish always seem bigger, the sun a little brighter. It doesn't matter. Funny how something simple like that can connect a father and his child. I guess a father has to actually care about their child to take them fishing. My Dad died a couple years ago. The doctors said it was liver failure. He drank himself to death. (beat) I wish I could say everything I just told you was true... but it wasn't. I made it all up. What a happy fish story that would have made, huh?

"A Happy Fish Story"

When I was younger, my dad and I used to go fishing… I miss those times. He'd wake me up and say, "Let's go! The fish can't eat until we get there!" I don't know why, but, I laughed every time he said it… I think that's why he did it. It's like it was yesterday… the sun was just coming up, slight chill in the air… God I loved it. We would sit there for hours sometimes, and never catch a thing. But it was okay, because I was with my dad.

Then one day, BAM! I get this huge tug on my line. I didn't know what to do! I think we were both surprised… there were actual fish in this pond after all. So, my dad grabbed hold of my shoulder and said, "Don't let go! Let's give your Mom something to clean." So, I fought with that fish… I wasn't about to let this one get away. Well, after what seemed like an hour I finally reeled that sucker in. It was beautiful. It was about this big (large hand gesture), well, maybe more like this big (smaller gesture). Anyway, I knew I made my dad proud that day. So, it doesn't matter.

Funny, something simple like that made us both feel so connected. My Dad died a month later. The doctors had no idea what hit him. He was just gone… with no explanation or goodbye. I miss my Dad. (beat) I take my son fishing now and one day, hopefully, he'll take his children. We're not wealthy people, so, it's not a ring or a watch… our family heirloom will have to be a moment, a really happy moment.

"Singled Out"

(Ending a good cry) - I have the worst luck with men... and I don't know why? I'm a good person, I really am. I see others happy. Happy couples, kissing and happy... everywhere. Why can't I get some of that action?! And FYI, get a frickin room already! Have some consideration for those of us that are lonely. Selfish bitches! I mean, I get it... it takes a little effort. I've tried everything; Facebook, dating services, chat rooms, singles clubs, church... flashing people in the parking lot. I cold call widowers listed in the obituaries. I've paid my dues.

And I'm not picky... the other day I went to the movies with a really nice guy... and as it usually works out, there was someone in my way. So, I asked Brad to suggest that this... person scrunch down in their seat. Well, he proceeds with "mu, mu, mu, mumu..." Oh my God! Move your huge head! Was that so hard?! Get a speech therapist. Days later, while he's still struggling to spit out the word "Move", I already moved on. It's always the same result... if they're "drop-dead gorgeous" and looking at me that can only mean one of two things, "taken" or "deadbeat"! Either way it's going to cost me. (Mocking male voice) "It's how I roll." Yeah, I'm sure it is. I hope I gave you syphilis, you loser!

And then, there are the ugly ones. I mean that's fine if your dog is at the vet... they cuddle too. But do they all have to talk about their mothers? And if it's not their "mommy", it's "yak, yak, yak" about their inflated ego... you know what that ends up meaning later on... tiny. There was this one guy... Hector, he was goin' all night... he wouldn't stop talking and I think he ate like a rotten chicken sandwich or something cause "halitosis-boy" was ripe! I was terrified... one kiss... salmonella poisoning. I don't have time for that. Anyway, maybe it's just me but I wish they'd all shut up. What was I saying? Oh yeah, I just want to be happy. If I'm willing to go through a self-inflicted, pain and discomfort induced frenzy of teeth whitening, weight loss, boob enhancement, and high heels... can't one, just one, be my "Mr. Right"? I mean, is it me?

"I'm A Liar"

I'm a liar. Let's start there. Now, if you choose to believe anything else I'm about to say well, then that's on you. It's a "trust" I've learned to steal not earn. It's a… developed lifestyle. (pick up the pace) Anyway, I feel the truth is both overrated and under appreciated… confusing I know. The truth is complicated like that. What I think I mean to say is, "Truth is demanded but tossed aside if it doesn't meet our 'approval'." So, I found a solution that works for everyone, I tell people what they want to hear. If they're fat, I compliment their noticeable loss of weight. If they're ugly, I see their beauty. But, let me back up. It started when I was about… oh, I don't know, I've used so many different ages… let's just say ten. I'd watch my older brother do something wrong and my parents would ask, "Did you do that?" He would tell them the truth and predictably get punished. I thought there must be a better way to do this. But, it wasn't just about staying out of trouble. It was about… everything.

As I grew older it… I became more sophisticated… my doctors have a different term they like to use… I wanted my family and friends to be happy, random strangers to feel good, my work associates to feel important. There's so much instant reward! (deep sigh) I guess I just wanted to be liked. I just wanted to be loved. (beat) No, that's not true… my parents loved me… I was loved. I'm so pathetic! I'm not a good person… even now I'm bending the hard facts to get some sort of approval. The real truth is, I don't even care what you think! It's just so easy. (grinning) I disgust me. I can be anyone, from anywhere, at anytime. It's amazing!! A cure-all for whatever ails you. But I suppose you can't fool yourself… (laughs) okay, yes you can… people do it all the time.

(slow the pace) Look, the short of it is, being deceitful seemed to be the easiest way to accomplish whatever goals I had… the goal was: to gain popularity, cash, favors, sympathy, the sky's the limit. Don't mistake what I'm saying… I can see they're fat and ugly. I'm just not a good enough person to tell them that. "Tact" takes too much energy. But, before you get all "judgmental" on me… I have a point; the next time you're asked a loaded question like "Do these pants make my butt look big" or something simple like "How are you", remember you're just as guilty because now you're talking my language... and if you don't believe that, well, you're just lying to yourself.

"Commitment Issues"

I love you. I want you to know that. We'll always be friends…
unless you don't want that… and I would respect your decision. I
want you to know it's nothing you did wrong… it's me. Your
perfect and that perfect someone is out there waiting for you…
it's just not me. (said with routine) Cue the tears, guilt, begging,
insults, slap, food to the body… and some are not above spitting.
And I still pick up the bill… they wonder why I left them, crap. But
I don't blame them… it's hard to lose something special,
meaningful. I get it… and I've gotten it, much fewer times than
I've given it, of course. The hard score is love interests -1, me -
28… over the past 5 years. I don't know if dying counts as
leaving me. It hurt the same. I've broken a lot of hearts… I know
that. I guess relationships are a lot like projects for me… they're
exciting to start but they don't hold my attention very long. I'm
clearly a better sprinter than long distance runner, blah, blah…
you get the point.

Which brings me to where I am today, though I do get a strange
sense of accomplishment and satisfaction from the closure and
control, I don't really like myself very much. I'm starting to think
maybe there's something wrong with me. Some might say…
have said… I might have a problem with commitment… and
come to think of it, possibly denial… they've said that too. When
my Mother left my Dad she said to me… "You're just like that
worthless, two-timing, shit on the couch in there. I pity the
woman that sets eyes on you. Dinner's in the frig!" And just like
that… we ate dinner and never saw her again. I was 8 years
old… that might have been a bit over the top at the time. It was
pretty emotional for us, my Dad couldn't stop smiling and I… I'm
afraid it may have triggered some things… psychologically I
mean. Maybe I blame the women in my life; I'm taking it out on
them, right? It's like a bad horror film, except I'm not killing them
just (beat) hurting them. That's not fair. But if leaving them first
keeps me from feeling like that scared little boy again… I'll leave
a hundred more. Besides, they deserve a lot better than me…
just ask my Mom.

"Selfish Bum"

I was lying down, the other day, taking in the breeze, smelling winter in the air… just people watching. I like to do that sometimes. Takes my mind off everything. And by everything I mean, simple stuff… what to eat, where to sleep, basics. I really don't have much to worry about anymore. I always wanted that. I always said, "If only life could be simpler". Be careful what you wish for. The genie-wish always comes with attachments.

Anyway, it hit me, I know when I lost it all but I'm not exactly sure when I became "that person"… the kind that drinks from the bottle instead of a glass? It does get the job done faster, I suppose. Doesn't make it any easier to look at myself in the mirror though. I had a good life once upon a time… a family, friends, and a great paying job; it was an excellent place to work. I was happy there. But (deep breath) that was then. I stopped caring about the details; niceties and amenities that made life better a very long time ago. It gets very crowded in my head. I don't have time for that. My current circumstances help me to stay focused on nothing. A glass is for someone with something to celebrate… I'm a bum. To be clear, I'm not homeless… it wouldn't be fair to the truly "homeless" to use that term on me. I'm a bum.

I didn't lose my family in a car accident, I didn't get fired, or lose my house… even my friends have reached out to me… a lot. The fact is, I woke up one morning, got dressed for work, stared at my sleeping wife and (tearing up) …and couldn't do it anymore. I walked right by my 5-year old… son. He was playing on the floor… he reached up for me and I just couldn't reach back. I'm not sure why… I keep waiting for it all to make sense. So, in the meantime, I'll eat from garbage cans, sleep wherever I get tired and watch the hundreds of people walk by each day who judge me, resent, pity, envy me… want to save me. There are so many that need to be saved… I just want to be left alone until I figure out what I'm supposed to do next.

"Out On A Ledge"

(look slightly over and down to your left as if speaking to a person who is looking out their window - arms out flat against the wall, balancing on a ledge) - I know at first glance I may not appear to be afraid of heights... but I assure you I am. That said, I'm more afraid of getting off this ledge and going back inside. That, in there... scares the hell out of me. If she finds me she'll kill me! She's nuts. She'll push me to my death for sure and all because I didn't read her mind. I don't know how to do that... why didn't God equip man with that ability so we could be better husbands and boyfriends? I don't know... it's God's fault I guess.

By the way, I really do appreciate you listening... I don't have many people I can talk to about this, especially right now. (looking down to the street) I dropped my cell phone. I think I'm going to be sick. (deep breaths - beat) It's moments like this that force me to think... they bring clarity to the situation. The situation being every month I'm terrorized by what used to be my wife. Very loving and wonderful woman... the one I married. It starts with a game of question and answer that you know you'll lose... it's designed for you to lose. "Honey" ...that would be me before the bashing begins... "Honey" interchangeable with "Idiot", Loser", "Man who let's me down", ...sorry I got off track. "Honey, could you help me with this"? It's a trap... saying "No" will get you the same exact results. So, why not just say "No"? Because we think it'll be different this time. Crazy! But the mind screwing, the horrible questioning is warm up... it's just sport before the insane emotional circus soon rears it's ugly, satanic head. So many feelings... and rage, so much rage. But I love her... that I'm clear on. I'm sure it can't be much fun for her either. I'm gonna go in... pretend I hurt myself. It always works.

"An Honest Reflection"

I need you to stop talking… please. Can you look at me for a second… or longer if you can stand it? Trust me, it hurts just as much for me to ask as it does for you to do it. (deep breath) Okay, here's the thing… you turned away from me so slowly it made it easy to pretend not to notice. I'll apologize… I'm sorry. I should have cared enough to ask why but I didn't. I know why… and I don't blame you. I don't think I've ever really looked at myself in the mirror before, not really. I did that today… I examined my face, my body and all the dangling parts attached. It was a long time coming but at least it all makes sense now.

I let you turn away because it was easier for me. You were always so charitable about the way you disapproved. Every time you stared at me I felt your discontent. I felt your disgust. It tore through my confidence the way standing next to you magnified it. Let's face it… even at my best I was never able to compete with your expectation of me. You're beautiful and determined and a bitch. All these years later you haven't changed a bit. I'm ugly, fat and lazy… and now I'm aware of it. "Lazy", by the way, isn't something I saw reflected in the mirror today, it's something I've seen strongly reflected in my attitude for years. I hated the person I saw standing there… I don't like what I see… and I know you don't either. (tears well up)

Don't worry I'm not going to cry… that would be pathetic. (beat) Did I mention you don't look at me anymore? But I get it, there's nothing here to see. It only hurts because I love you… not what we had together… you. I'm not blind; you're hot as Hell (small laugh at the attempted humor). (Pause) I was ready to believe that I'm good enough for you… that's why I looked in the mirror you know. It was worth a shot. Hey, you win some you lose some.

Chapter 3

Show Me Something

Approximately 20 to 30-Second Monologues

Explanation & Use:

I refer to these as "Party", "Elevator" or "Show Me Something" reads. They require the skilled actor to show quick depth of character, and a focused ability to find "It" right on the spot... as more and more casting directors are asking the trained actor to demonstrate. No one wants to hear a long dragged out rendition of Shakespeare when they're in a hurry. There's no better calling card to showcase your talent when only a few moments are allowed... let's say, in an elevator for example. Seize the moment!

Tip! When put on the "spot", as actors often are, remember to center yourself and be passionate. All anxiety aside, this shouldn't require much effort if you truly love acting and want to work. Passion and enthusiasm can easily be found and used, in any situation, to make the moment more believable. Impromptu opportunities often require the actor to pull from what he/she knows best... self. Show them what you're made of!

Know yourself and what you want for your character; it leaves less room for others to fill in the blanks. It will also help you to make honest choices for your character without bias or reservation
- Steven G. Lowe

"Obvious Secret"

I have a secret... yeah, that always gets some attention. Wanna know what it is? If you look close enough I won't have to tell you. But that's the problem isn't it? You don't look anymore.

"Thank You Mom"

I fell today... not from grace or anything that dramatic, just off the step of my front porch. It was a small ride down... but when I hit the ground (tearing up) I remembered my Mom and how she used to comfort me. She always knew how to make me feel better. I've always been able to get back up because of her.

"Every Now & Then"

Do you ever have conversations in your head? I do. I think it's starting to happen more than usual too. I really go at it... in my head. You know, weird stuff sometimes. (laughing) If people could hear what's going on up there they'd think I was crazy. (laughter lessens, slightly nervous, honest) I think I might be crazy every now and then.

"Memories Of Dad"

When I was younger my dad and I used to go fishing... I miss those times. He'd wake me up and say, "Let's go! The fish can't eat until we get there!" I don't know why but I laughed every time he said it... I think that's why he did it... I miss my Dad.

"Alone & Me"

I woke up this morning, about 3 a.m., gasping for air. I was soaked with sweat and trembling... I felt this overwhelming feeling of fear and anxiety like I had never felt before. I wanted... I needed someone to be there for me. What an incredible sense of loneliness.

"Human Spirit"

Can one word define the human spirit? If so, then it should only take a second to explain my actions. If not, then there's not enough time. There will never be enough time. I'm sorry.

"Defining Moment"

I remember thinking, if I can just get through this moment everything will be fine. But no matter how hard I tried (taking a breath and exhaling hard) I just couldn't do it... I just let it all slip away. That moment defines me now... and I don't know how to fix it.

"Frozen With Fear"

I heard the noise from behind me and I froze. I didn't turn around... I didn't try to run. I don't know why but I just stopped. I was so scared. How does that happen to someone my age? I just remember being scared. Then... nothing.

"First Time"

I was young. I sat on the bed waiting. My stomach felt like it was in my throat, my whole body was tingling, and I was mess. It was about to happen after all this time; wondering what it would be like... this was it. Yes! I finally got cable TV in my room.

"Rationalizations End"

Yeah, I let him hit me once. You get that one for saying you "love" me. Then he hit me a second time and I thought, "I deserve that one for believing you." By the third and fourth hit... I ran out of rationalizations and shot his ass ("His ass" can be replaced with "him" according to your preference).

"Christmas Reprieve"

I went Christmas shopping early this year... I love to shop. I'm an over-gifter. This year I had a bit more motivation; there was a (pause) greater sense of urgency (phone rings, stare at the number calling in - raise cell phone - pause) Yes this is. (joyful emotion fills your face - lower phone and put away). Looks like I'll have more time to wrap gifts then I thought. (under breath) Yes.

Chapter 4

Quick… But Effective

Approximately 30 to 60-Second Monologues

Explanation & Use:

Agents, casting directors and managers often request a monologue of this length for the purpose of seeing how quickly an actor can find their character and depth of emotion… and, of course, when time is limited. These are also in the "Show me something" family and are becoming more and more popular. What a great way to demonstrate what you can do with little time! If they're to be done right, contrast or a layering of emotion must be present. Nothing this short is worth seeing, or performing, if it's portrayed flat and without strong purpose. In short, let emotional distinction carry the words and you'll be exactly what they hoped for. This length is also great for the aspiring beginner in private coaching and group classes.

 **Tip!** Emotional availability is key! When layering two combating emotions always remember to choose the stronger more apparent emotion as your foundation. Then it'll be easier to sprinkle in the other emotion where it's appropriate. This is also true for emotions you find harder to maintain. For example: If the two layered emotions were sadness (resulting in tears) and joy, you may find it easier to focus on sadness as a base so you can express your momentary joy with a well placed smile and eye energy… never leaving us unaware that you're still hurting.

Being prepared is the best way to equip yourself for success
- Steven G. Lowe

"Conflicted In Death"

Well, if you're watching this it means "I've gone"… (slight laugh) and I don't mean on vacation. Nope, I've given up the ghost, passed away… I'm dead. It's a harsh reality we'll all have to face one day. (beat) I've never sugarcoated anything and I'm not going to start now. You are a horrible person but I love… loved you. The crazy thing is, I never wanted anything while I was alive but now that I'm dead, I want more time with you.

"The Harder Question"

I want to tell you about my first time… it went something like this; they held me down and told me, this is the way it's going to go… do you understand? What kind of question is that? What was I supposed to say, huh? What, did they want permission? So, I let it happen. (beat) I ask myself everyday why I didn't choose the knife… I wish I had chosen the knife.

"Sisters"

I've looked at you everyday for the past week wondering if you're ever going to tell me. Do you know how hard it is for me, knowing? (beat) But I knew what you'd say if I asked, "What are you talking about? You're overreacting… as usual." Please, don't say that… please don't do that to me. We're sisters, you're my best friend. You're hurting me. (beat) Why'd you have to do this? Can't you see everything is wrecked now? I hate you for that. I really hate you! I really love you.

"So I'm Dying"

So… I've always been known as the strong one. It's who I am, I guess. (beat) I'm dying. The doctor called me today… (slight smile) I shouldn't have picked up the phone. (tears well up) The truth is I'm not as strong as you might think, in fact… I'm really scared. It's kinda funny don't you think? *(Proper delivery of the last line requires knowing what they find funny or embarrassing about their plight, i.e. - that they're crying/scared).*

"Queen Of The Damned"

You made me feel like I was everything. You made me believe
that I was special. (Pretends to cry then starts laughing) Yeah
right. The best thing that ever happened to me was you leaving.
You're a bitch! Seriously, someone should have rammed a stake
in your heart years ago because you are without a doubt Queen
of the damned! And now I'm free.

"Self-Preservation"

"The instinctive need to survive danger"… self-preservation.
What's the word, or phrase, for when you just don't fight back
anymore? I'm not weak or a coward or depressed. Maybe
exhausted is the right word. I don't know maybe I'm even a little
bored with it all. Sometimes the fight is too big to care about. It's
so much easier not to care… it's overwhelming. And again, I'm
not depressed. So, the only choice I'm left with is flight because I
know I won't survive the fight… problem is, I've never run from
anything in my life. See my dilemma? I realize it's my life I'm
talking about here. I don't have a death wish (slight laugh at the
thought). Realist! That's the word!

"The Motivator In Need"

Few things move or shake me… not the way most people are.
The way I see it: problems come and go… life happens and we
can choose to get stuck or we can move on. My mantra is, be
confident, be strong, be… more than you are. You better believe
it's all about positioning and it is all subjective. If you view
yourself as the small man in the room then let your handshake
be sweaty. If the problem is bigger than you, then it simply is.
(sad, worn down) Well, (beat) today was simply a big day. How
do I tell the people that look up to me, to be "more"… you know,
for them… that I'm just not up for it today? (putting a big smile on
your face) Hear that? All that applause is for me. I have to go on
now… they need me.

"Miserable Goodbye"

It's sad. You're just like everyone else: all talk and empty promises. I know how much you hate it when I say that... but I'm mad... and you deserve it. You felt things... like I do. I needed you to be miserable with me... you promised! Who did you think you were impressing? I don't care, remember?! It's part of my charm. You were the only one who knew me and still liked me. I have so many feelings inside of me right now... I'm a serious mess. I hate everyone! I want to blame everything! I want to text you about it. You didn't impress me... you're so stupid! I told you not to drive but you never listen. (beat) I don't want to be miserable alone.

"Distant Love Dance"

I saw you smile today... your dimples are so cute and you know it, don't you? I melt when I see you. I can't take this smile off my face. I used to feel lonely... all the time. But then you came along and changed everything. My life has meaning, maybe for the first time... (slight laugh) who am I kidding, definitely for the first time. How do I begin to thank you for the times we've shared? They're beyond words. How lucky I am to have found you. I can't think of anything else but you. I wonder... do you know I'm there? Do you feel my presence? I see you glance and my heart races, it jumps and I'm alive. The rush is incredible! How can one person have that much control over another? I love you. Tonight's the night.

"Distant Love Dance - Part 2"

Have you ever felt like someone's watching you? I know it
sounds crazy but I've been so freaked out lately and I don't know
why. Sometimes I get goosebumps for no reason... my skin
crawls and I'll shiver like, I don't know, like an icy breeze just
blew through my body or something. My friends think it's weird
so I just laugh it off... they're probably right. My boyfriend said I
have cheerleader-itis; I need to imagine people are staring at me
even when I'm alone. (laugh becomes concerned) I know it's
stupid but I'm a little scared. I think I'll just drop it now before all
my friends think I'm nuts. (a breath) hmm. Oh, one last note from
the creeper file; that nerd was at the grocery store again today. I
caught him looking at me. I thought he was going to piss himself.
He's strange but harmless... I'm sure it's nothing.

"Distant Love Dance - Part 3"

I see you watching me. My friends think I'm paranoid, I thought I
was crazy. Every shadow, every noise... but you slipped up last
night and I'm glad you did. I saw you staring through my
bedroom window... looking down at me like your prize
possession. (transition from semi-scared to a big smile) I liked it.
You thought I was sleeping... fooled you. (slight laugh) I was
actually watching you watch me... and all my fear went away.
How do ya like me now? I get it, no wonder you watch for so
long... it's (beat) strong. I felt in control. I'm not the timid victim
anymore. I really thought you'd be a monster but you're just as
scared as I am... and no offense, my imagination was so much
more frightening than you. I have a few questions of my own
now: How long have you been watching me, what have you
seen? Are there others? Because that would really make me
jealous. I may have to do a little snooping of my own... game on
creeper.

*You have the right to succeed. Never give up on your
dream. Just be realistic about the approach.*
- Steven G. Lowe

ABOUT THE AUTHOR

As an accomplished acting coach and Talent Manager, Steven G. Lowe has been helping actors develop their strengths and conquer their limitations for over a decade. As the Founder of The Actor's Room, television and film workshops in Los Angeles and Orange County, California, Steven has helped to shape the careers of many notable actors. Recognized by many as one of the industry's leading personalization coaches, Steven's insight and technique have become known worldwide, gaining him the respect of his actors and many top professionals in the entertainment business. Steven is the Co-Founder of Last Chance Productions. As a Production Executive and Screenwriter he has a vast experience in film and television development. In the early years, Steven applied his creative talents to radio where he established himself as an on-air personality, producer and voiceover artist in a series of worldwide radio-syndicated shows.

What truly separates Steven from other coaches is his ability to blend over 20 years experience in the film/television/radio industry with 25 years of counseling at-risk youth and their families (specializing in human behavioral observation). This exceptional talent combination is translated into his writing, seminars, scripts, and coaching.

Steven's diversified and extensive background has given him an amazing understanding of the inner workings of the acting world and a genuine ability to educate with a refreshing and honest approach. Steven believes an actor's individual creative process must be respected, ultimately encouraging the performer to achieve autonomy. Whether coaching one-on-one or by written teachings, Steven helps his actors find purpose.

"My desire is to please God, motivate others to achieve what they love, and to eat a great meal!"
- Steven G. Lowe, The Actors Room

www.ingramcontent.com/pod-product-compliance
Lightning Source LLC
Chambersburg PA
CBHW070035110426

42741CB00035B/2778